TABLE OF CONTENTS

Introduction

Chapter 1: Understanding the Basics of Websites
    Why Websites Are Important
    Common Misconceptions About Websites

Chapter 2: Understanding Domain Names
    What Is a Domain Name?
    How Domains Work
    The Process of Buying a Domain
    Register Domain Name
    WHOIS Information

Chapter 3: Understanding Domain Name System (DNS)
    How DNS Works
    DNS Caching
    Difference Between Domain Registrar and DNS Hosting
    Common DNS Record Types
    Using DNS to Point a Domain to Hosting
    DNS Propagation and How It Impacts New Websites

Chapter 4: Web Hosting Basics
    Types of hosting
        Shared Hosting: A Great Starting Point for Your Website
        What are the benefits of shared hosting?
        How does shared hosting work?
        What are the limitations of shared hosting?
        Why is shared hosting so popular?
        VPS Hosting: A Powerful and Flexible Solution
        More resources, more flexibility
        Scalability and reliability

Affordable and powerful

VPS hosting is perfect for

- Websites that need more resources and flexibility

- Businesses that expect sudden spikes in traffic

- Those who want more control over their website's performance

- Anyone who wants a reliable and scalable hosting solution

Hosting features to consider

    Uptime Guarantee

    Support Options

    Security Protections

    Scalability Options

Choosing a hosting provider

    Identify Your Needs

    Research Various Hosts

    Utilize Comparison Tools

    Consider Long-Term Needs

Signing up for web hosting

Chapter 5: Building Your Website

Content Management Systems

Using Templates and Themes

Customizing and Updating Your Site

Understanding HTML and CSS Basics

Difference Between WordPress.org and WordPress.com

Chapter 6: Going Live and Beyond

Promoting Your Website Launch

Reaching The Finish Line

Extras and Glossary

Introduction

The internet has revolutionized the way we live, work, and communicate. But for many, the technical side of websites, domains, and hosting remains a mystery full of confusing jargon.

Many books about how to build a website start with a certain expectation. They say, "Pick a registrar, buy your domain, buy your hosting, now let's build your website."

There you go, quick as a wink, you are in like Flinn.

I realized the first time I had this conversation on the telephone with a customer:

> "Good morning, BlahtyBlah Hosting; how can I help you today?"
> "Hi, my name is Curly McCurlcurl," Curly replied, "I just set up an account with you guys, but I don't see my website yet. What's going on with that?"
> "What is the domain name that you set up? Did you get a free domain from us, or did you buy one someplace else?"
> "I signed up for an account."

"Alright then, we are happy to have you with us. When you started the account, there was a line that said, 'What domain name would you like to use?'. What did you put there?"

"I put in 'curly.com,' but that didn't work. I tried a bunch of things, but nothing worked, so I said I wanted to use something else."

Thus began a Wednesday morning.

This book breaks down the complex world of web technology into simple, easy-to-understand language.

In Tech Talk Decoded: Websites and Hosting, we'll start from square one to cover how websites work and build a foundation of web knowledge.

You'll learn the step-by-step process of registering a domain name, choosing a hosting plan, building a site, and getting it online. Along the way, we'll decode the terminology around DNS, URLs, HTML, CSS, and more, so it all makes sense. (I can't guarantee that it will make complete sense, but you will know more.)

By the end of this book, you'll know how to register your domain, set up professional email addresses, build an essential website, troubleshoot problems, and understand web hosts.

You'll learn the difference between WordPress.org and WordPress.com, point your domain to a hosting account, and choose the best web host for your needs and budget. No prior experience is required!

With this beginner's guide, you'll gain the confidence to create an online presence.

Let's get started demystifying the world of web technology together. That way you can get your "online presence" started.

Chapter 1: Understanding the Basics of Websites

Websites have become an integral part of our daily lives. We use websites for everything from news and entertainment to shopping and managing finances.

However, many people don't understand the basic concepts behind websites and how they work. This chapter will cover why websites are essential and common misconceptions about them.

Why Websites Are Important

In the digital age, websites have become essential for individuals and businesses. They provide a platform to showcase products or services, connect with potential customers, and establish credibility in an increasingly competitive market.

A well-designed website offers convenience for consumers by providing information at their fingertips and allows businesses to reach a larger audience.

Furthermore, websites contribute to building brand identity and recognition.

With carefully curated content, branding elements such as logos, color schemes, and fonts can be integrated into the site's design, creating a cohesive visual experience that reflects the essence of the business.

This helps establish trust and ensures customers can easily recognize and differentiate your brand from competitors in today's crowded digital landscape.

Moreover, websites offer invaluable data insights that can drive business growth. Through analytics tools like Google Analytics, website owners gain access to valuable information about their visitors' behaviour patterns - such as how they found your site or what pages they spend most of their time on.

This data informs businesses about trends and preferences among their target audience, enabling them to make informed marketing decisions tailored specifically to their consumer base.

Websites are powerful in today's digital age. They enable businesses to expand their reach, establish credibility through branding efforts, and gather crucial data insights for decision-making.

Embracing this online platform is no longer optional but essential for anyone looking to thrive in today's tech-savvy world.

Common Misconceptions About Websites

Misconception #1: **Websites are extremely complicated and require coding skills.**

> While early websites did require some HTML and coding expertise, today's site builders, content management systems and easy drag-and-drop interfaces allow anyone to build a website without technical skills. Solutions like WordPress and Squarespace empower beginners to create polished, professional sites.

Misconception #2: **You need to hire a web developer and spend thousands.**

> Professional web developers provide valuable services, but aren't always practical or in the budget for small sites. DIY site builders make it possible to create sites independently and cheaply. Shared hosting starts around $5-$15 a month for basics. With WordPress and Joomla content management systems (CMS) there are

multiple tutorials and classes that would allow a self made site to have a wide range of functionality that previously had to be custom developed. Even without the time investment of classes a great site can be built with CMS themes and extensions or plugins.

Misconception #3: **Websites require constant updates and maintenance.**

Websites do need maintenance and security updates, but not daily oversight. With a good host and a content platform like WordPress, Joomla, or Drupal, to mention a few, todays websites can hum along smoothly without intensive upkeep. Good planning and design on the frontend reduces workload down the road.

Misconception #4: **I don't need a website I have a great Social Media platform that I use.**

Not everybody believes this, but I have seen it enough to worry about it. The number one drawback to using a social media platform to build your business is that, well quite honestly, that traffic doesn't belong to you as the business owner, blogger, or average person. It takes one misplaced social post to have your account suspended. You don't have a mailing list, or a list of customers, you have social followers. Guess what happens when the media platform suddenly decides that your type of business has fallen from the graces of their "approved" businesses. OR, you make the mistake of wording a post in a way that they don't approve. Has there been a review of the terms of service? What might I say that can cause my social media account to be temporarily suspended, or worse, banned. If it hasn't happened yet, I am truly happy. At any time, the traffic that has been so beneficial can be shut off. I heard a comment recently: **If you are using a product that is free, then you are the product.**

This beginner's guide will walk you through getting your first website online, from registering a domain to choosing hosting to building a website using a platform like WordPress, Joomla, or another CMS (Content Management System), or even just plain old HTML.

With the right preparation and knowledge, you can successfully create and manage a website, even without technical expertise.

The following chapters will demystify the jargon around domains, DNS, hosting, and content management so you can confidently join the online world.

Chapter 2: Understanding Domain Names

What Is a Domain Name?

A domain name is a key part of any website. The unique web address identifies your site and brand on the internet. For example, "example.com" is a domain name.

When registering a domain, you will purchase the registration through a company called a "registrar". This allows you to do pretty much anything you want with that domain until that registration is over. It is very much similar to a lease of a name. The money costs range anywhere from free (yes there are some places that provide a free domain while you use their service) to $20 per year. The average that I pay through Dynadot, my personal favorite Registrar, is $10.19 (2024). The domain becomes how customers find your site online, so it should represent your business or site purpose.

How Domains Work

Domains operate on a registry/registrar model. Registries manage the reservations for each top-level domain (like .com or .net). Registrars are companies authorized to sell domains to customers, interacting with the registries behind the scenes.

For example, Verisign serves as the registry for .com and .net domains, ensuring their uniqueness, accessibility, and security. While I primarily register domains through Dynadot, a trusted registrar, it's important to note that Verisign operates in the background, guaranteeing that each domain is securely registered and globally accessible. Verisign plays a crucial role in the internet's infrastructure, particularly for widely-used domains like .com and .net, which remain among the most popular and trusted extensions available.

Common TLDs (Top-Level Domains):
-.com - Most popular for businesses and sites
-.net - Often used for networks and technical sites
-.org - Used by nonprofits and organizations
-.info - General informative sites
-.biz - Normal for small businesses
-.uk, -.ca, -.us, -.au - These are country-specific domains and sometimes require a presence or citizenship in that country to purchase.(More information about country codes can be found on wikipedia.org, here is a link for that article https://t1m.pw/countrytlds.)

New domain extensions are being added, it seems, every day, providing more options. With these additional TLD's as of April 2024, the choice of Top-Level Domain (TLD) like .com, .net, .org, or an alternative TLD (such as .info, .biz, .online, etc.) does not inherently disadvantage a website in terms of Search Engine Optimization (SEO) purely based on the TLD itself. Google and other search engines have stated that generic TLDs do not receive special treatment over newer TLDs in search rankings. **The primary focus for search engines is on the relevance, quality, and value of the content to the user, not the website's TLD.**

(Trigger Alert! Information you may not need, but, if you are nerd/geek/technonut it's fun to know. Skip if you want. Too many words, too many details.)

The Governance of Domain Names

If you have ever purchased a domain name from a registrar, you may have seen something about an "ICANN" fee, which is in 2024, $0.18 of the cost of any domain.

If you have a domain already registered, you may get a notice from the registrar saying that "ICANN is increasing domain pricing." So what the heck? Who is this "ICANN" and why do you care? (Other than, of course, the fact that pricing goes up because of a fee from them.)

ICANN (the Internet Corporation for Assigned Names and Numbers) charges an annual fee of $0.18 for each year of domain registration, renewal, or transfer. (As of January of 2024.)

So now, you have seen the name "Verisign" and "ICANN" and everybody has a specific point of governance. So what do they each do, and how do they work? The registrar is the intermediary between you, the domain owner and the ruling powers that be.

Roles and Responsibilities:
- ICANN: ICANN is a nonprofit organization responsible for coordinating the maintenance and procedures of several databases related to the namespaces of the internet, ensuring the network's stable and secure operation. ICANN oversees the allocation of IP addresses, management of the root server system, and the policy-making for top-level domains (TLDs).
- VeriSign: VeriSign, on the other hand, is a private company that provides a range of internet infrastructure services, including domain name registry services and internet security services. VeriSign is best known for operating two of the internet's thirteen root nameservers and for being the authoritative registry

operator for the .com and .net TLDs, under contracts with ICANN. This means VeriSign is responsible for the registration and administration of all domain names that end in .com and .net, ensuring their resolution on the internet.

Nature of the Organization:
- ICANN: A nonprofit and multi-stakeholder organization that involves representatives from governments, commercial entities, technical communities, and civil society in its decision-making processes.
- VeriSign: A for-profit, publicly traded company that operates as a business providing domain registration and internet security services.

Functionality in the DNS:
- ICANN: Does not directly deal with the registration of domain names with end-users but instead coordinates the overall framework and policies within which domain names are registered and managed. It delegates the responsibility to various registrars and registry operators.
- VeriSign: Directly involved in the technical operation of the .com and .net parts of the domain name system, ensuring that domain names within these TLDs are accessible from any location worldwide.

(Triggers ended, moving forward only moderate trigger potential.)

Choosing Your Ideal Domain Name

Choose your domain strategically. It makes a first impression and represents your brand identity online.

When brainstorming your ideal domain name, you may find the exact match is already registered. Don't worry - there are strategies to find an alternate available option.

One approach is to use a thesaurus to find synonyms and related words to your first choice. For example, if "techblog.com" is taken, look up synonyms for "tech," such as "technology" or "computing." You can also try variations like "mytechblog" or "thetechblog."

A thesaurus helps you generate fresh ideas when your first domain pick is unavailable so you can find a similar name to represent your brand. Be open to creative variations.

The goal is to register something memorable that aligns with your site identity.

Now most of the Registrars have some type of domain suggestion tool incorporated into their domain search.

If there are still no suggested domain names that entice you, I would suggest using an Artificial Intelligence (AI) tool. These are all the rage now and will include apps like ChatGPT (offering a free and a paid version), Claude (also, having a free and paid version), Gemini (Google), Llama (Meta/Facebook) and others are top lovel AI tools. Then there are things that are composite tools like Perplexity and OpenRouter.ai, both of which have become strong contenders, that use multiple AI tools to generate ideas.

Don't infringe **trademarks, copyrights, or patents.**

When choosing a domain name, it's crucial not to infringe on existing trademarks or copyrights. This means you should avoid domains that use brand names, logos, or other intellectual property belonging to established companies.

Even if a domain is technically available, registering it could still be less than wise, and though I am not an attorney, barrister, or law languagist, it could be less than legal.

For example, Nike.com clearly cannot be registered by anyone but Nike. Any usage of trademarks in a domain could lead to legal action. Do research to ensure your domain choice does not already have associated legal rights. (I may not be an attorney, but I do know when you might need one. Just be aware of what you are doing here.)

Your safest option is to brainstorm original names and words representing your brand rather than borrowing from others. This will minimize any potential disputes or allegations of trademark infringement.

Here is a table with links to some country trademark registration websites. I don't know if these will provide instructions to find the trademarks, but this should get you started. This is not exhaustive, and will only be for a few English speaking regions.

Nation	Link

Unite States	https://t1m.pw/usatm
Canada	https://t1m.pw/canadatm
United Kingdom	https://t1m.pw/uktm
Australia	https://t1m.pw/australiatm
European Union	https://t1m.pw/eutm

The Process of Buying a Domain

1. Brainstorming names that fit your brand.
2. Comparing domain registrars, my personal favorite is Dynadot.com. I don't belong to their affiliate program, if they have one, but they are easy to use, and don't try to sell you something else when you click on something.
3. Searching availability of domains (https://www.dynadot.com/ is an example)
4. Purchasing a domain for up to 10 years at a time.
5. After purchasing the domain, "point" it to a hosting account. This is done by adding "nameservers" to the domain registration. (We will go through that later.)

Register Domain Name

When you register a domain name, you typically do so for a set registration period, usually 1-10 years. Once that period is nearing expiration, it's important to renew your domain name on time to maintain control of it. If you fail to renew the domain before the expiration date, it will lapse and become available for anyone else to register.

Most registrars will send renewal reminders, but be sure to calendar your domain expiration date and renew at least several weeks in advance. Renewal can often be done with just a few clicks. If you already have auto-renewal enabled, no action is required with most registrars. Keep in mind that it doesn't remove the responsibility of ownership from me/you as the owner of the domain.

Keeping your domain renewed ensures the registration stays in your name uninterrupted. Allowing it to expire accidentally could mean losing that web identity you've worked so hard to establish.

WHOIS Information

Your contact information is stored in the WHOIS database when registering a domain name. WHOIS is a public record that lists the registrant details for every domain.

This includes the name, address, phone number and email of the person or company that registered the domain. Some domain registrars offer "private" registration to mask your information, but there is sometimes an additional yearly fee for this privacy service. (Sometimes ½ of the price of the actual domain registration, if not more. Dynadot does not charg for this privacy.)

By default, your WHOIS information will be visible to anyone searching your domain name in the WHOIS database. This allows people to contact the owner of a domain if needed.

Make sure the email you provide when registering is one you actually use and check regularly. When I first started buying domain names I had to spend $35 to buy the domain name and they didn't even offer the option to have privacy added (This was in 1995). It was like the old phone company in the USA, where you had to pay a monthly fee to NOT be listed in the phone directory, and you couldn't buy your telephone, you rented it from the phone company. At that point in time in my domain buying life, when you registered a domain name, each and every domain name had your personal information listed. It tended to generate a lot of telemarketing calls eventually, from web service companies wanting to build you a website, or handle your marketing.

About Publicly Available Information:

When registering a domain, there are typically three types of contacts that are required for the domain registrar: Administrative Contact, Technical Contact, and Registrant Contact. These are all needed for domain registration and may or may not be displayed for the public. Each of these types of contacts serves different functions:

> **Registrant Contact:** This is the legal owner of the domain. This contact holds the rights to use and, if applicable, sell or transfer the domain. It's crucial information because it identifies the person or organization that has legal ownership and ultimate authority over the domain. The registrant contact is considered the rightful, legal, owner.
>
> **Administrative Contact:** This contact is authorized to answer questions about the domain and make important decisions. This can include making changes to the domain name's registration, transferring the domain, or updating any relevant information. While not having the legal ownership like the registrant, the administrative contact is crucial for day-to-day management and is often someone who works on behalf of the registrant.
>
> **Technical Contact:** This is the individual or group responsible for the technical aspects of

managing the domain, such as the DNS configuration and resolving technical issues. They handle the technical operations of the domain but do not control the legal or business aspects. This contact is crucial for maintaining the website's functionality, email, and other services associated with the domain.

These roles can be filled by different individuals or entities to ensure a separation of duties, which is especially important in larger organizations for security and efficiency. However, in many cases, particularly with small businesses or personal websites, the same person or entity might fill all three roles. The separation allows for smoother operation, clearer responsibility delineation, and enhanced security by limiting access based on roles.

There is a way to contact domain owners should one wish to purchase a domain, without using an auction to find it. Generally, when searching for a domain name, if the domain is taken, nearly all domain registries will have a button that says something like: "Make Offer", for most domain names.

https://www.dynadot.com/domain/search

So all in all, if the domain name is taken, you can either make an offer of at least $199, or you can move to another domain.

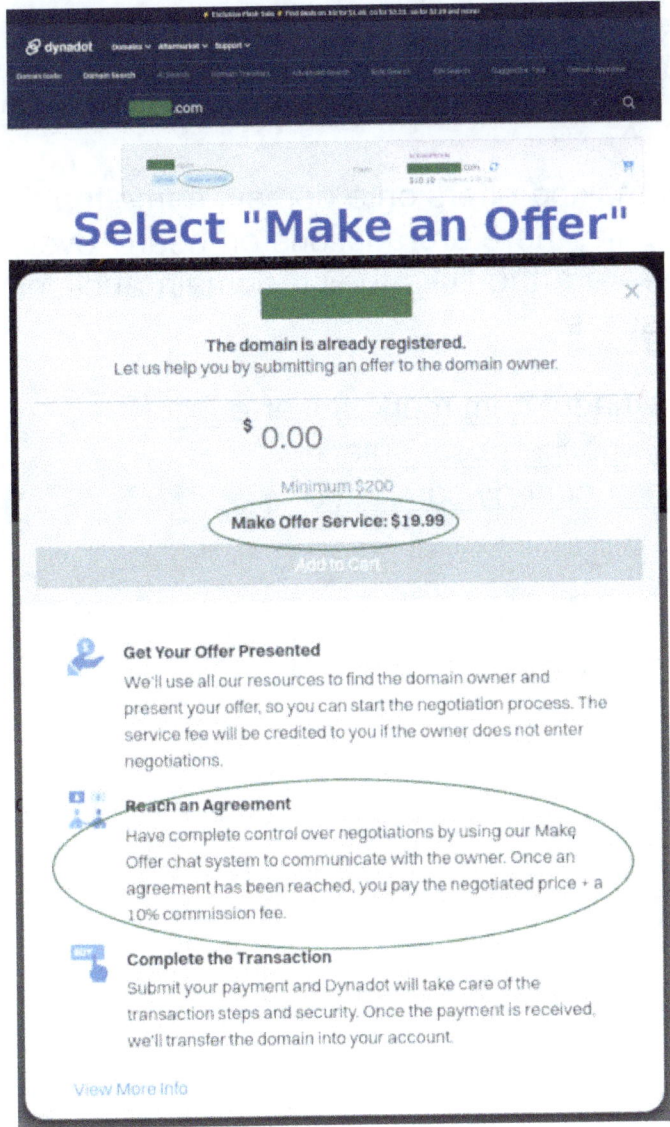

In checking into buying an existing domain name, I found, that in addition to buying the domain for a minimum of $199, there is of course the brokers fee, of $19.95, plus a 10% commission.

Should a specific domain name be critical to the plan that you have then it is by all means worth the money.

In addition to making offers on a domain name that is not listed for sale, there are auctions on nearly every registrar. Here are the links to find domain auctions on some registrars:

https://www.dynadot.com/market/user-auction
https://www.namecheap.com/market/
https://auctions.godaddy.com/beta

Chapter 3: Understanding Domain Name System (DNS)

Now that you understand how domain registration works, it's time to dive into the critical behind-the-scenes system that runs the internet - the Domain Name System or DNS.

DNS is like the phonebook of the internet, translating domain names into IP addresses. It is a complex globally distributed database that connects users to websites.

While technically it is backend functionality, DNS is relatively straightforward from a user perspective. When registering a domain, you assign **nameservers** to it. A nameserver is a crucial component of the internet infrastructure. It is responsible for translating domain names which people understand (such as www.example.com) into IP addresses (such as 123.123.123.123) so that computers can understand.

When you type a domain name into your web browser, the nameserver is queried to find the right IP address to direct your computer, allowing your computer to connect to the correct server and load the website. Nameservers play a vital role in ensuring that internet traffic is directed to the correct destination.

Nameservers will be automatically added to your hosting account, whether you host with a registrars hosting or with another web hosting environment. These servers hold records that route traffic for that domain. By modifying DNS records, you control how your domain name resolves, think of it as telling the various parts of the domain name where to be found. It makes it easy to change the website hosting.

This chapter will cover the basics of how DNS works, common DNS record types, choosing DNS hosting, and using DNS to connect your domain to a website. Understanding DNS is key to properly configuring your domains to work as intended.

Let's demystify DNS and learn how it bridges the gap between domain registrations and live functioning websites!

How DNS Works

DNS works through a hierarchical distributed database system. That is kind of a mouthful, but here is another way of looking at it:

Imagine DNS as the internet's phonebook, but unlike a single, centralized directory, it is spread out globally. This is similar to having different sections of a phonebook located in various offices around the world rather than in one big building. Thus, it is considered a distributed system.

The organization of this system is not random but structured much like a family tree, hence the term "hierarchical." There's a top-level guide that directs you to more detailed guides, which in turn lead you to even more specific ones, just as you might follow a set of instructions to reach a particular department in a large corporation.

When you want to visit a website, DNS functions as your navigator, moving through this structured network of guides from the most general down to the specific, ensuring that your computer can find the exact internet address you're seeking. This system allows everyone, everywhere, to locate precise information quickly and efficiently, much like using a well-organized reference system to find a specific topic in a library.

At the top level, root name servers store information about the Top Level Domains (TLDs) like .com and .net. These TLD servers then delegate to lower level name servers that contain records for individual domain names.

When you type a domain in your web browser, your computer sends a query that navigates this hierarchy starting at the root. The request filters down through the layers of DNS servers until it reaches the authoritative name server for that domain.

This server has the IP address information needed to route the domain to the correct hosting location. The IP is sent back to the original requester, allowing the browser to load the site. This whole recursive process happens invisibly in milliseconds.

Occasionally one area or server stack may be off line, when that happens the traffic is delayed for a short period of time. Most of the time, as the backups for the backups for the backups re-route, it is not something a "patient" person will even notice. Chances are that when there is a delay, it's not going to be because of the nameserver connections, it's going to be because of the local connection to the internet, or the webhosting server is down. At least in most of the world, it is really a reliable system.

DNS Caching

DNS caching plays a key role in speeding up the domain name lookup process. (Caching can be considered a "temporary" memory, something that is easily and quickly accessed.)

When a DNS server receives a request for a domain name, it will first check its cache to see if it already has a record of the IP address associated with that domain. If it finds a cached entry, it simply returns the IP address back to the requester. The browser then heads to the address given to show the pages of the website.

This allows it to bypass going through the full lookup process. It is also worth noting that your web browser has a cache facility that assists with the speed of this process.

DNS cache entries expire on a defined time-to-live (TTL). However, popular domain IPs may stay cached for longer. This is why, sometimes, when building a new site, the old site shows up without showing the most recent bunch of changes. DNS servers also leverage a shared cache to distribute cached records across different servers.

Together, this caching system reduces the number of full recursive lookups a DNS server has to perform. Instead of navigating the DNS hierarchy for every request, the server can pull the IP address from cache for faster performance.

Statistics show a DNS cache hit rate of over 90% for most servers. Caching is a core optimization that allows DNS to handle billions of requests per day without significant delays. It maximizes speed and efficiency in the search for the correct server to find the website you are looking for.

Difference Between Domain Registrar and DNS Hosting

Domain registrars and DNS hosting providers perform separate but related roles when it comes to websites.

Domain registrars handle registering and renewing domain names. When you buy a domain from companies like Dynadot, Namecheap, or Godaddy, they are the registrar. However, registrars don't always host the DNS records for a domain, they will point any requests to the appropriate nameserver. They will tell any requestor, "oh yeah, we sold that to somebody and they are keeping it here." They store the nameservers and direct traffic to the correct server. Consider the registrar as the street sign for the domain names that they sell.

DNS hosting refers to the management of the Domain Name System (DNS) for a particular domain name. It involves configuring the name servers and DNS records that control how a domain name is resolved to an IP address.

Many registrars include basic DNS hosting for domains registered with them. But advanced users often use third-party DNS hosting services like Cloudflare, AWS Route 53, and NS1. Most of these have free tiers of service and professional services that are available for a fee. It is best to visit these sites individually and read their documentation. Usually for beginning website owners these third party vendors are not going to be the best solution. Usually your first website will have maybe five to ten records required. There may be more, and if they are needed someone is going to have to have more information that this book is prepared to teach.

The "normal" DNS records that are needed are as follows:

NameServers (or nameservers, or Nameservers, I think that the debate on the correct spelling is still being fought):

ns2.dyna-ns.net.
    sillycrazyname.vip
ns1.dyna-ns.net.
    sillycrazyname.vip

A records are the simple IP address that tells servers how to get to the site:
    192.187.xxx.xxx
        sillycrazyname.vip
    192.187.xxx.xxx
        www.sillycrazyname.vip
    192.187.xxx.xxx
        cpanel.sillycrazyname.vip

MX records are the email servers for the domain name.
    20 mx2.zoho.com.
    10 mx.zoho.com.
    30 mx3.zoho.com.

The full DNS record does have a tendency to become very complicated very quickly and it can generate issues as simple as "why does my website look different when I type 'www" at the beginning" "My website doesn't work". Some are quite easy to solve and figure out, but other times it is considerably more complicated.

Registrars register and sell domains, DNS hosting providers store and manage the records that make domains work. You register your domain name via a registrar, then set up DNS hosting with them or a separate provider. The registrar and DNS host work together to connect your domain registration to functioning DNS records. For a beginning website I do recommend that using the nameserver associated with hosting is the simplest solution.

Should you be using GreenGeek.com, where TechTalkDecoded.com is hosted, use the nameservers:
    ns1.greengeeks.net
    ns2.greengeeks.net

This means that if you use a2hosting.com, one of my favorite shared hosting platform use the following nameservers:
    ns1.a2hosting.com
    ns2.a2hosting.com
    ns3.a2hosting.com
    ns4.a2hosting.com

If using siteground.com use:
    ns1.siteground.net
    ns2.siteground.net

Common DNS Record Types

There are several key DNS record types that serve important functions:

- A records - The fundamental DNS record that maps a domain name to an IP address. This points the domain to a web server hosting the website.

    So if you type in the URL cpanel.sillycrazyname.vip it will go to that 192,187.xxx.xxx IP address. (Until I change server addresses.)

- CNAME records - Used to create an alias for a domain name. For example you could make www.example.com a CNAME that points to example.com.

CNAME	imap	sillycrazyname.vip
CNAME	mail	sillycrazyname.vip
CNAME	pop3	sillycrazyname.vip
CNAME	www	sillycrazyname.vip

  - By typing www.sillycrazyname.vip you will be directed to the sillycrazyname.vip website, which, by the way is 192.187.126.194.
- MX records - Direct emails to the right servers by mapping domain names to mail server IP addresses. You will only need to do this if you select to purchase a domain named email e.g.

john@example.com. If you decide to use example@yahoo.com, you will not need to setup an MX Record. However, it is worth mentioning that a yahoo email account is not as professional as a domain registered email account.
  - If you get a hosting account with a2hosting.com, bluehost.com, siteground.com or most other hosting providers, you will be able to set up an email account with your domain name. You can also invest in email hosting from Google, Zoho, Microsoft, and a multitude of other providers.
- TXT records - Allow you to store text notes and data in DNS records. Often used for email authentication.
- NS records - Name Servers identify the domain to the rest of the world. The phone book of the internet. Designate the name servers hosting DNS records for a specific domain zone.

There are many other record types, but A, CNAME, MX, TXT and NS records handle the most common DNS capabilities needed for managing domains and email.

Understanding these core record types allows you to control your DNS set up.

Using DNS to Point a Domain to Hosting

The primary way to connect your domain name to your hosting server is by setting up an **A record**. The A record maps the domain name to the IP address of the web server that is hosting the website files.

For example, if you purchase hosting at A2Hosting.com, you would login to your DNS management console and create an A record for "www.yourdomain.com" that points to the IP address of your A2Hosting.com hosting account. This ties your domain name to the hosting server's IP address.

Now when someone types your domain name into their browser, the DNS lookup will find the A record and direct the traffic to your hosting server at A2Hosting.com. The IP address acts as the bridge between the domain name and hosting provider.

Configuring the A record is essential to getting your domain name working with your hosting. The A record can be seen as not only the street name but address and the apartment number where it can be found on the server.

DNS Propagation and How It Impacts New Websites

When making DNS changes like pointing your domain to new hosting, it takes time for the updates to propagate worldwide. DNS records are distributed across many global servers. So when you make a change, it must spread to all servers globally before taking full effect.

This propagation process usually takes 24-48 hours to complete. Until it does, some users may still see the old DNS records for your domain instead of the new configuration. This has become a much quicker process over the years, frequently it is almost instant. However, the more importance there is on a quick response, the more likely it is to take the 24 to 48 hours. DNS is one of those things that remind me of something my Grandmother used to say, "A watched pot never boils". Of course she also said, "Never marry a girl who doesn't like tomatoes." So I know that it may not apply to tech, but don't be surprised if it takes longer than expected.

For new websites especially, this means the site won't load immediately for everyone right away. DNS changes need time to fully propagate globally.
Some users may get an error at first while waiting for the DNS records to update across all name servers.

If you have just purchased your domain name, why does it show up for you so quickly? I have had people ask "I can see it, why can't Mom see it? She only lives in the next town over?"

Quite simply, your computer knows where it is. Your computer was there when you set it up. It is cached in your local "dns resolver". It may even be cached in your service provider's DNS resolver. If the internet provider uses the same source resolver then it's customers may see it. Your domain will be registered and then things will be reported up and down the chain of nameservers, starting with the root servers. It's quite an elaborate system. It's simple, but it does take a little bit of focus to understand. It also takes, here it is, from 24 to 48 hours for it to go up the chain and down the chain.

That's why when launching a new site, it's smart to point your domain to hosting a few days in advance if possible. Most hosting platforms have "temporary" URLs for you to access to allow you to build your site prior to having the domain go to the actual real URL. This gives time for DNS changes to propagate so all users will see the new site immediately on launch day.

Chapter 4: Web Hosting Basics

Now that you understand how to register a domain and configure DNS, the next building block is web hosting. Hosting is what physically stores and serves your website files to visitors.

Just as a house requires land to exist, a website needs hosting set up before any content can go live. At its core, a web host provides the actual server space where your site will reside.

This chapter covers the fundamentals: the different types of web hosting, how it works, and key features to consider when selecting a hosting provider.

We'll explore the most common types of hosting, including shared hosting, VPS, dedicated servers, and specialized platforms like WordPress hosting.

By the end, you'll be prepared to choose the best web host for your needs.

With domain and hosting established, you'll then be ready in the next chapter to start building and launching a website.

Let's delve into the world of web hosting!

Types of hosting

Here is an overview of common hosting types:

Shared Hosting: A Great Starting Point for Your Website
Shared hosting is a popular and affordable way to get your website up and running. It's like sharing a house with roommates - multiple websites live together on the same server, sharing the same resources. This setup is perfect for small websites, personal blogs, and new businesses that are just starting out.

What are the benefits of shared hosting?
* **It's cost-effective**: Shared hosting is one of the most budget-friendly options available, making it a great choice for those who are just starting out or have a small online presence.
* **It's easy to use**: Shared hosting is a great way to start because it's easy to manage, even if you have no technical experience. You don't need to worry about complicated technical setup or maintenance.

* **It's flexible**: Shared hosting can accommodate a wide range of websites, from small blogs to larger business sites.

* **It's a great starting point**: Shared hosting is a great way to get started with your website, and you can always upgrade to a more advanced hosting platform later if you need to.

How does shared hosting work?

Imagine a big server that's divided into many smaller spaces. Each space is allocated to a different website, and they all share the same resources, like CPU power and memory. This means that you'll be sharing the server's resources with other websites, but don't worry - reputable hosting companies like A2 Hosting have systems in place to ensure that each website gets the resources it needs.

What are the limitations of shared hosting?

While shared hosting is a great option, it's not perfect. There are limits to the resources you can use, and if you start to use too much, you may need to upgrade to a more advanced hosting platform. Additionally, some hosting companies may offer "unlimited" resources, but this can be misleading - there are always limits to the amount of resources you can use on a shared server.

Why is shared hosting so popular?

The majority of new websites are hosted on a shared hosting platform because it's a great way to get started. It's easy, affordable, and flexible, making it a perfect choice for those who are just starting out or have a small online presence.

VPS Hosting: A Powerful and Flexible Solution

Imagine having a dedicated server all to yourself, but without the hefty price tag. That's what VPS (Virtual Private Server) hosting offers. With VPS, you get a virtual machine that's dedicated to your website, but shares the same physical server with a few other websites.

Think of it like a condo

In shared hosting, multiple websites are crammed into a single "apartment" (server), with limited resources to go around. But with VPS, you get your own "condo" (virtual machine) with its own dedicated resources, like a private kitchen and bathroom. This means you have more control over your website's performance and can make changes without affecting other websites.

More resources, more flexibility

VPS hosting provides more resources, like CPU power, memory, and storage, than shared hosting. This means your website can handle more traffic and sudden spikes in popularity without slowing down. It's like having a larger kitchen to accommodate more guests.

Scalability and reliability

With VPS, you can easily upgrade or downgrade your resources as needed, giving you more flexibility and scalability. Plus, since your website is isolated from others, you're less likely to be affected by their traffic or security issues.

Affordable and powerful

The best part? VPS hosting is still relatively affordable compared to dedicated hosting. You get the benefits of a dedicated server without the hefty price tag.

In short, VPS hosting is perfect for:

- Websites that need more resources and flexibility

- Businesses that expect sudden spikes in traffic

- Those who want more control over their website's performance

- Anyone who wants a reliable and scalable hosting solution

Dedicated Servers: The Ultimate in Website Hosting

Imagine having a powerful computer all to yourself, dedicated solely to running your website. That's what a dedicated server is.

With a dedicated server, you get a physical machine that's entirely yours, not shared with anyone else. This means you have complete control over the server's resources, allowing you to customize and optimize it to meet your website's specific needs.

Unlimited Possibilities

Unlike shared hosting or VPS, a dedicated server gives you full access to all of the resources and capabilities of that server. You can install any software, configure any settings, and allocate resources as needed. This means you can handle massive amounts of traffic, run complex applications, and store large amounts of data without worrying about running out of space or power.

Security and Reliability

A dedicated server also provides enhanced security and reliability. Since you're the only one using the server, you can implement advanced security measures to protect your website and data. Plus, with a dedicated server, you're less likely to experience downtime or performance issues, ensuring your website is always available to your visitors.

Ultimate Flexibility

Dedicated servers are ideal for websites that require:

* High traffic volume
* Complex applications or software
* Large data storage
* Customized configurations
* Enhanced security

With a dedicated server, you get the ultimate flexibility to run your website exactly as you want, without any limitations.

Cloud Hosting: A Super-Flexible Way to Host Your Website

Imagine you're running a lemonade stand, and suddenly, a huge crowd of thirsty people shows up. You need to make more lemonade, but you don't have enough cups or sugar. That's kind of like what happens when a website gets a sudden surge of visitors. (Like when your lemonade stand wins a Super Bowl or World Cup television advertisement.)

Cloud Hosting is like having a magic lemonade stand that can instantly grow or shrink to match the demand. It's like having an unlimited supply of cups, sugar, and lemons, so you can make as much lemonade as you need, whenever you need it.

With Cloud Hosting, your website is hosted on a network of powerful computers that can be scaled up or down instantly. This means that if your website suddenly gets a lot of traffic, the cloud can automatically add more resources to help handle the load. This way, your website can handle the surge of visitors without slowing down or crashing.

The best part is that you only pay for what you use. It's like only paying for the cups and sugar you need, rather than buying a whole bunch of extra supplies that might go to waste. Cloud Hosting services like Amazon Web Services (AWS) Lightsail or Google Cloud Platform usually bill by the hour, so you can adjust your resources as needed and only pay for what you use.

This makes Cloud Hosting perfect for websites that are growing quickly or experiencing sudden spikes in traffic. It's like having a flexible, magic team of helpers that can scale up or down to meet your needs, so you can focus on running your website and making delicious lemonade (or whatever it is you do!)

Some additional notes about Web Hosting

The storage capacity and bandwidth available on a web hosting server directly impacts how much traffic a website can handle. Servers have finite disk space and data transfer allowances.

When all the allocated resources are used up, additional visitors will be unable to reach the site until traffic volumes decline or additional capacity is added.

That's why when choosing hosting, it's important to consider not just your current space and bandwidth needs, but also future expected growth.

Undersizing your hosting means you are more likely to eventually max out limitations and crash your site under high traffic loads. Oversizing too much leads to unnecessarily high costs.

Understanding your expected traffic growth allows properly sizing your server space and bandwidth to accommodate current and future viewers in a cost-effective way.

This keeps your site stable and accessible even during periods of peak demand.

Plan ahead so your hosting can scale in line with your goals for expansion.

Hosting features to consider

Uptime Guarantee

When looking for a web host the higher the uptime guarantee the better. Many offer 99.9% which is great, and really amounts to about 2 minutes of downtime potential per day. (Quick math shows that is up to an hour per month, which is for the month, not per day.)

The advertised uptime is going to be related to the server, and not necessarily to the site accessibility. There can be network outages beyond the control of the hosting company. Just because your site is not accessible to you, it does not mean that your website is "Down". If you can still get on the internet, and your site can't be seen by you, go to "https://downforeveryoneorjustme.com/", and enter your site name. Generally, unless there is something going on at your web hosting company, your site may not have a problem at all.

Support Options

When searching for a web hosting company, considering the support options they provide is crucial. Here are some key factors to keep in mind regarding support:

1. 24/7 Availability
   Look for a web hosting provider that offers support 24 hours a day, 7 days a week. Website issues can arise at any time, and having access to support whenever you need it is essential to minimize downtime and resolve problems quickly.

2. Multiple Support Channels
   A good web hosting company should offer various support channels, such as live chat, phone support, email, and ticketing systems. This allows you to choose the most convenient method for you to reach out for assistance.
3. Response Time
   Consider the average response time of the support team. You want a hosting provider that can address your concerns promptly. Look for reviews or testimonials from existing customers to gauge the efficiency of the support team.
4. Technical Expertise
   The support team should consist of knowledgeable and experienced professionals who can provide accurate and helpful solutions to technical issues. They should be well-versed in the hosting platform, common web technologies, and troubleshooting techniques.
5. Knowledge Base and Tutorials
   In addition to direct support, a comprehensive knowledge base, FAQ section, and tutorials can be invaluable resources. These self-help options enable you to find answers to common questions and resolve issues independently, saving time and effort.
6. Community Forums
   Some web hosting providers offer community forums where users can interact, share experiences, and seek advice from fellow customers. These forums can be a great source of information and support, as well as a way to learn from others' experiences.

7. Scalability of Support
   As your website grows, your support needs may change. Consider whether the hosting provider offers scalable support options to accommodate your future requirements, such as dedicated account managers or premium support plans for high-traffic websites.

   By evaluating these support aspects, you can choose a web hosting company that not only provides reliable hosting services but also offers robust and accessible support when you need it most. Responsive and knowledgeable support can make a significant difference in your overall hosting experience and the success of your website.

Security Protections

When searching for a web hosting company, it's crucial to consider the security measures they have in place to protect your website from various threats. Here are some key security precautions to look for:

1. Firewalls
A robust firewall is essential for protecting your website from unauthorized access and malicious traffic. Look for a hosting provider that offers a web application firewall (WAF) to monitor and filter traffic between the internet and your web application, blocking potential attacks like SQL injection and cross-site scripting (XSS).

2. DDoS Mitigation

Distributed Denial of Service (DDoS) attacks can overwhelm your website with a flood of traffic, causing downtime and disruption. Choose a hosting provider that offers DDoS protection to detect and mitigate these attacks, ensuring your site remains available to legitimate users.

3. Malware Detection and Removal

Malware can compromise your website's security and harm your visitors. Look for a hosting provider that offers automatic malware scanning and removal services to keep your site clean and secure.

4. SSL Certificates

SSL (Secure Sockets Layer) certificates encrypt the communication between your website and visitors' browsers, protecting sensitive data like login credentials and payment information. Many hosting providers now offer free SSL certificates, such as Let's Encrypt, to secure your site.

5. Backup Frequency and Retention Policies

Regular backups are crucial for protecting your website data in case of a security breach, hardware failure, or accidental deletion. Consider the backup frequency and retention policies offered by potential hosting providers. Look for daily or even real-time backups, with multiple restore points to minimize data loss.

6. Other Security Measures

Additional security features to consider include:
- Intrusion Detection and Prevention Systems (IDS/IPS) to monitor network traffic for suspicious activity
- Two-factor authentication for enhanced login security
- Security audits and penetration testing to identify and address vulnerabilities
- Automatic security updates for your content management system (CMS) and plugins.

By choosing a web hosting provider that prioritizes these security precautions, you can significantly reduce the risk of threats like data breaches, malware infections, and DDoS attacks. Don't hesitate to ask potential providers about their specific security measures and how they can help protect your website and its visitors.

Server Processing Power (CPU)

The CPU handles all the processing and logic on the server. Look for hosting plans with fast, multi-core processors that can efficiently handle many simultaneous requests, especially during traffic spikes.

Some top options include:
AMD servers with 32 CPU cores for power and security
Intel Xeon E3 servers for durability, scalability and memory efficiency
Dedicated servers with up to 16 cores and 20 threads for maximum performance

Caching
Caching stores copies of files to deliver content more quickly without having to re-request it from the origin server each time.

There are a few main types of caching to leverage:
Browser caching - stores site files on the visitor's local machine
Server-side caching - saves data on the server using a CDN, reverse proxy, or in-memory key-value store like Redis

Object caching - stores database query results to avoid repeated lookups
Opcode caching - stores compiled PHP code to speed up execution

WordPress sites can easily implement caching via plugins like WP Super Cache, W3 Total Cache or WP Rocket.

These handle tasks like minifying code, caching database queries, and integrating a CDN.

Content Delivery Network (CDN)

A CDN distributes your site's static content across a global network of edge servers. This places content closer to visitors to reduce latency and load times.

Look for a CDN with:

Many global PoPs for broad coverage
Easy integration with your CMS or via a plugin
Support for the latest protocols like HTTP/2 and Brotli compression
Security features like WAF, DDoS protection and SSL/TLS

Cloudflare and Stackpath are popular CDN options that check these boxes. Many hosts also offer integrated CDNs powered by providers like Cloudfront or Fastly.

Optimized Database

The database stores all your site's content and settings. Slow queries can bog down performance. Optimize by:

Choosing a host with fast SSD storage and ample RAM for caching

Cleaning up old data, spam comments, post revisions, etc.
Optimizing tables and adding indexes to speed up lookups
Using a caching plugin to avoid repeated queries
Upgrading to a higher-tier plan if the database exceeds 1-2 GB

Web Stacks & Platforms

Certain web stacks and platforms are designed for speed. For example:
NGINX + PHP-FPM for fast, dynamic content
Node.js for real-time apps and APIs
Static site generators like Hugo, Gatsby or Jekyll
Google Cloud, AWS, or Azure for auto-scaling cloud infrastructure
Many managed WordPress hosts use these stacks along with server-level caching and a CDN. WP Engine, Kinsta, Flywheel are some speedy options.

In summary, maximizing your site's speed requires the right combination of robust server resources, smart caching strategies, a global CDN, and an optimized database and web stack. Choosing a performance-focused host that provides these pieces out-of-the-box is often the simplest path to a faster site that ranks well and keeps visitors engaged.

The importance of speed and processing is not necessarily an early decision. It is more like an early awareness for a website owner. As traffic and visitors increase and the size of the website gets larger there may come a time to improve performance, and there are definitely ways to do that. This is all sort of "back of mind" things that a website owner should think about.

Scalability Options

Can disk space, bandwidth transfer, and other resources scale seamlessly as your site grows over time? Vertical and horizontal scaling allows for expanding hosting capabilities on demand. Starter packages can generally cope with tens of thousands of visitors at once without extending beyond the limitations.

As mentioned earlier, unless you have an incredible following or an amazing budget to get early traffic to your site, a standard shared account will suffice for most blogs initially. Your site will grow and extend beyond the capacity of that shared account, but it won't likely be on a single day. There will be a ramp up period. Then all of this information will come in handy.

Choosing a hosting provider

Identify Your Needs

Start out by thinking about the following list of criteria:

- What's your budget? Remember the purpose of the site. If it is just a way to share your life, and you don't expect revenue, lowest cost is probably fine.
- Will you be running affiliate offers, or selling a product? Do you need a storefront? Maybe your content (blog, pictures, sales information) should go in one hosting platform and your store could go on something like BigCommerce or Magento.
- Will you be using a content management system, like Joomla, or WordPress?
- How much traffic do you project getting?
- How will people find your website? Will you rely on organic search, Instagram, Facebook, maybe your YouTube channel? (organic search is when somebody types in something like

Research Various Hosts

Search for hosts specializing in your platform (WordPress, Joomla, Drupal, or Magento, etc) at your budget level. Compare pricing, features, performance, support rankings and reviews across top contenders.

Utilize Comparison Tools

To really dig into the various comparisons of website hosting there are numerous options. Here are the two recommendations that I have for new website developers.

1. Visit a website that explains how and why they make their picks for hosting. I have used or maintained websites on most of these hosting platforms in their top 10. I just signed up for a Hostinger account, and I am using it for a website right now. The other one I have never used is Nexcess hosting. I have used all of the other eight platforms and have a lot of experience with all of them
This article provides excellent information and also it explains their methodology for making their recommendations.
https://websitesetup.org/top-web-hosting-services/
(*Just as a notice, if you click on the link to any of these websites on that page they will most likely get a commission. I'm not positive that they will, but if they aren't they are missing out. It doesn't cost you any more for them to get that referral fee.*)
    a. I like the fact that they have tested the various hosting platforms and report on downtime and speed of the sites. In order to test the platform they have actually bought and used their webhosting services.
    b. Some of their "facts" seem good, but their conclusions are a bit in error, in my opinion. Follow closely here:

i. Hostinger: (Best all-round hosting) Over a recent 12-month period, the average uptime of Hostinger was 99.95% based on our tests. There was also a total downtime of 3 hours and 33 minutes
ii. Bluehost: (Best uptime hosting) Through this year-long test, it was found that the average uptime was 99.91%. The total downtime was 5 hours and 31 minutes. It does seem a bit odd that their "Best Uptime Hosting, had two hours more downtimes than the Best All-Round Hosting.
iii. A2Hosting: (Best speed hosting) Our test results show that the average uptime was 99.98%, and the total downtime was 70 minutes. This would, in my summation, be the Best Uptime.
c. They present a lot of data on this website, including speeds of the websites that they put up. The speed of the website is determined by a website called "pingdom.com" which is a great tool for measuring most of the things that you need to measure for a first time website.

2. Try the hosting platforms that you are interested in trying. There are, however, some drawbacks with that plan.

a. This could get expensive. For example a signup for 2 years with Hostinger is $2.87/month for 24 months ($68.88 for 24 months). If a somebody wants to try a one month option the cost would be $11.99 for the first month. Most states now charge a sales tax on web hosting.
b. A one or two month tryout of a hosting company may not provide a fair representation of what a user may need to see. (Besides being nearly a fifth as much of an investment for the 24 month plan.)
c. Trying out multiple hosting options would require multiple domain names and also sites that are pretty much the same in all regards. Images per page, image sizes per page and the content of those pages would need to be similar at the minimum.
d. I have seen many things happen with hosting companies that change their performance. Even this level of research and testing can change overnight.

Consider Long-Term Needs

Choose a provider positioned to grow with you through flexibility, performance guarantees, managed scaling abilities and excellent support. Don't lock yourself into limited servers or long-term contracts.

Hosting providers offer great discounts for signing up for a 12 to 36 month hosting agreements. These introductory hosting costs for longer terms can be considerably less than their regular monthly pricing. The advantage of this type of hosting agreement is that after a few months, it becomes a break-even cost factor that would make it conducive to moving your hosting should it become necessary. This also allows a customer to decide what they like and what they don't like about the structure of the web host that they are using.

The hosting market has an incredible number of options, but thoroughly comparing providers makes finding the ideal balance of affordability, features and quality for your specific needs achievable.

Signing up for web hosting

1. Purchase a Domain Name

In my personal experience, when a host offers a free domain, it may not be the best thing to do if it's a domain that you want. There may be others who argue this, "Why look a gift horse in the Mouth?". A free $10 to $15, why say no to that. A domain name can have the nameservers changed every day, I don't recommend that, but if it's not in your name you can't move it to your name for the first 60 days after it has been registered, with only a few exceptions.

Understand what their policy is about their free domains. Do you own the domain if you cancel, or if you take advantage of their hosting cancellation policy? The money is nothing if you don't have the brand that you have built you whole concept around.

Just purchase your own domain name, you can then easily point it to any web host you desire. Your new web host will provide you with name servers to allow your site to be visible on their server. In the appendix, I will walk you through setting up the domain in three different registrars dashboards.

2. Choose Your Hosting Provider

Compare multiple hosting providers based on budget, features, reliability, and reviews to select the best solution for your site goals and needs. While I have discussed multiple sources above, the following is a list of the top 25 web hosting providers offering shared web hosting accounts.
- **A2 Hosting** - High speed and reliable uptime.
- **GreenGeeks** - Eco-friendly with robust hosting features.

- **Hostinger** - Competitive pricing with solid performance and features.
- **SiteGround** - Known for excellent customer service and reliability.
- **DreamHost** - Affordable, unmetered traffic, and free domain.
- **InMotion Hosting** - Good for eCommerce and high-speed storage.
- **iPage** - Affordable with essential features for beginners.
- **1&1 IONOS** - Good for eCommerce with competitive pricing.
- **Web.com** - Easy to use for beginners, comprehensive packages.
- **HostPapa** - Great for small businesses with excellent support.
- **Namecheap** - Affordable with good performance and support.
- **TMDHosting** - High performance and reliable uptime.
- **FastComet** - Good global reach with strong customer support.
- **AccuWeb Hosting** - Reliable with good customer support.
- **InterServer** - Budget-friendly with consistent performance.
- **ScalaHosting** - Strong security features and high performance.

- **JustHost** - Good for simple sites with solid uptime.
- **Arvixe** - Feature-rich with good performance.
- **Liquid Web** - Excellent for businesses needing high performance.
- **WP Engine** - Best for managed WordPress hosting with top-tier performance.
- **Kinsta** - Premium managed WordPress hosting with excellent speed.
- **Cloudways** - Flexible cloud hosting with excellent performance.
- **HostGator** - Affordable, with extensive support resources.
- **Bluehost** - Popular for WordPress sites, beginner-friendly with good support.
- **GoDaddy** - Largest domain registrar with reliable hosting.

At the top of my list to personally recommend are the following:

A. GreenGeeks - I have talked to people who have been involved with this company since it started, and I have used their services. As a matter of fact the website for this book is hosted on GreenGeek.com. This company is very conscientious and helpful.

They are about as carbon neutral as they can be, and they like to do the right thing, even when nobody is looking.
I belong to the Greengeek affiliate program:
Link from the e-book:
https://www.greengeeks.com/track/baldman
Less typing if in the hard copy:
https://t1m.pw/greengeek

B. A2Hosting - has served me well for several years, and has done right by customers that I have suggested using their hosting. Their servers are very fast and even on shared hosting, it's very reliable.
I belong to their affiliate network because in my experience this is one of the three best hosts to use for shared hosting services.
The link from the e-book:
https://www.a2hosting.com/?aid=baldman&bid=945ee523
Less typing if in the hard copy:https://t1m.pw/a2hosting

C. Please notice the webhosting companies at the bottom of the list. I have used the top five, and the bottom three on this list. The bottom ones are there for a reason. If you were to look at rankings though, they do rank amongst the top. It is not for reasons that I am able to discern.

I do not recommend the last three webhost companies on that list. I have found that the best way to use those three companies is as names to fill out a list. All three were good at one time, but that time has past, in my experience. I have not used Hostgator since 2015, Bluehost in 2023, Godaddy unfortunately quite recently with devastating results for a client of mine.

3. Select Hosting Package

Decide which one is the right type of hosting to start with. To review, there are shared, VPS or dedicated server configuration based on projected storage space needs, monthly traffic, sites hosted, and growth expectations. Scalability should be a consideration. However it should not be the only consideration.

I would recommend that picking a small package, usually in the middle of the pack for shared hosting is a great starting point. The reason that is my recommendation is because the introductory offer is usually for hosting only one domain name.

Let's look at greengeeks.com hosting:

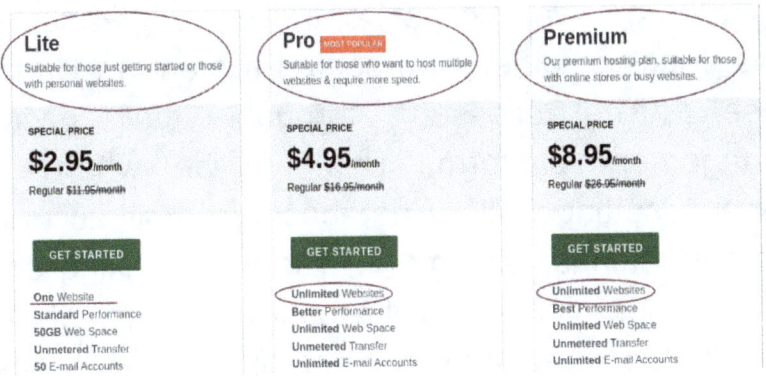

Let's check out a2hosting.com:

4. Add to Cart & Purchase

Once hosting package selections are complete, add to your cart and complete purchase. Payment confirms the order, and you should receive an email confirmation with your login information.

5. Access Control Panel

Login to your web host's Control Panel (cPanel, site tools, Plesk or other web control systems). Usually, these are accessed through the account management platform. This will be where you manage settings, files, databases, email accounts, domain settings, and more. It is worth taking some time and learning about the control panels, whether for your account management or for your website management.

6. Set Up Site Files & Databases

For a new site, the content management system may or may not be installed when setting up your account. Not to fret, this is a simple process at most web hosting companies. They usually have a software installation application, like "Softaculous" or something similar that makes a content management system a breeze to install.

Most of your files, for content of your site, can be uploaded through the CMS once it is installed. This limits the need for extra steps trying to log into an FTP server or uploading through the control panel upload process. I do however recommend that you set up an FTP user account on the system, and explore the site with an FTP tool like Filezilla or CuteFTP.

If moving an existing website to a new web host, some hosts will migrate a limited number of websites for free. Or some backup plugins in WordPress just install CMS platforms like WordPress, upload website files, and handle other foundation setup steps in the control panel. This is generally the time that most folks get to know the support team of their new hosting platform.

Chapter 5: Building Your Website

With your domain registered and web hosting established, you now have the essential building blocks in place to start creating an actual website.

This chapter explores popular platforms, themes, and methods for building out and customizing the content and structure of your site.

We'll cover the basics of the leading content management systems like WordPress, and Joomla which make building websites easy even without coding expertise. Selecting visually appealing themes and customizing layouts and features is also important for maximizing impact. We'll discuss some additional resources for basic HTML and CSS knowledge which can help with modifying templates more extensively.

By the end of this chapter, you'll have plan to move forward. What should you include on your website? How to map out that content. Will you use a CMS platform? We will walk through common hosting tools to install that CMS and what parts there are in a CMS. We will have some common settings as well as how to set them.

WordPress is said to be the preferred platform for nearly 45% of all websites on the internet. We will discuss what makes it as easy as pie and I might just say some things that make the WordPress fans angry enough to burn this book.

We will talk about developing individual pages and posts in WordPress. What are some content best practices, and some of the accessibility considerations that are important in today's litigious environment. Let's get hands-on now with how to build your fully-functioning website!

Content Management Systems

Content Management Systems (CMS) are the core platforms for building dynamic websites today without needing to program everything from scratch. Rather than coding thousands of lines of HTML and PHP manually, CMS software handles most of the heavy lifting.

CMS options handle site setup, templates, layouts, admin dashboards, community integrations, security protections, and more. This empowers anyone to build an attractive, feature-rich site through pre-made modules and a few clicks.

Popular CMS Platforms

WordPress - Focused on blogging originally but now used to power over 40% to 45% of websites from personal to enterprise level. Wide range of plugins, themes, integrations and hosting options exist. It is very SEO friendly.

Joomla! - Powerful, flexible CMS geared towards multi-lingual sites, eCommerce stores, directories, social networks and complex web apps. Steeper learning curve but very customizable code-wise.

Drupal - Robust enterprise open source CMS with strong community support. Ideal for building more advanced websites like multinational corporations, universities, governments and non-profits.

Below is a table outlining the features, advantages, and disadvantages of WordPress, and Joomla:

Feature	WordPress	Joomla
Ease of Use	User-friendly interface is very easy to comprehend	User-friendly admin area and very well documented

	Easy installation and setup	Easy to navigate for beginners
	Large community support	Quick learning curve for basic use
Customization	Vast selection of themes and plugins	Extensive extensions and templates
	Easily customizable without coding	Customization options through modules
	Great for small to medium-sized sites	Good for medium-sized websites
Community Support	Largest user base and community	Active community support

	Abundant online resources	Dedicated forums and documentation
Performance	Generally good can be fine tuned for better speed and usability	Performs well for medium-sized sites
	Can be affected by poorly coded plugins	Performance may vary with extensions
Security	Regularly updated for security	Security features and extensions available
	Popular target for hacking due to popularity	Security is very strong because of the different structure of the integrated coding.
Scalability	Well-suited for small to medium sites but is used for more sizeable sites that can afford developers	Scales well for medium to large sized projects

	Plugins may affect scalability	Suitable for growing websites
Cost	Open source and free	Open source and free
	Additional costs for premium themes and plugins	Some extensions may require investments for licenses
Ideal Use Cases	Blogs, small to medium websites	Small to medium-sized business sites, or corporate intranets
	Content-heavy sites	Community websites

Please note that the information provided here is a generalization, and the suitability of each platform depends on specific project requirements and user expertise.

The choice comes down to feature needs, capabilities, ease-of-use, flexibility and ecosystem of themes/extensions available. All make professional sites more achievable even without programming expertise.

Generally speaking, a content management system should be simple for the site owner or developer to use and manage. It could be found that the number one CMS is not the one that will build your site. I encourage people to try a couple of them.

It's fun to learn, and to see how many new words a person may use to vent their frustration. The easily installable CMS platforms on the webhosting platforms are free to try. I do however recommend that the learning section be a limited time, so that progress can be made.

Using Templates and Themes

One major benefit of CMS platforms is the ability to easily customize the design and appearance of your site using pre-made templates and themes. You don't need any design or coding skills to leverage them.

What are templates and themes?

Themes control the overall aesthetic design like colors, fonts, and layouts site-wide. Templates can be the same as themes but may focus more on internal organization and elements within individual pages. Hundreds of free and premium options exist.

Finding Themes & Templates

In CMS admin panels or their communities (like WordPress.org) you can browse, preview, and install themes/templates with one-click. Filter by criteria like features, industry, rating, and more to zero in on matches.

Customizing Designs

Most templates and themes come with customization options to tweak colors, fonts, widget areas, page layouts through the CMS without touching code. You can easily arrange layout containers and enable/disable integrated site building blocks.

For deeper personalization, modifying the underlying HTML/CSS source code directly allows advanced users to finely tune alignments, padding, responsive breakpoints and visual hierarchy. This requires some specialized coding knowledge. I personally wouldn't recommend learning some of the customizations skills with coding in any of the CMS tools out there. People don't go to most website for the stunning beauty of the site. Visitors want the information that you have.

Leveraging pre-made templates and themes accelerates launching beautifully designed sites. And customization settings empower further enhancements to align the aesthetics with your brand.

Customizing and Updating Your Site

CMS platforms provide many built-in options for customizing your site to match your brand, without needing to code, such as:

- Change colors, fonts, layouts via theme settings
- Add/remove site sections and pages
- Modify individual page templates
- Embed multimedia content
- Create reusable content modules
- Select menu structure
- Configure slideshows, galleries, feature sections

For deeper changes, developer documentation from platform communities outlines how to:

- Edit source code (HTML, CSS, JavaScript)

- Install third-party plugins
- Integrate APIs (Forms, Payments, Live Chat)
- Manipulate the database behind the scenes

Updating Your Site

To keep your site running optimally, be sure to regularly:

- Install CMS software updates for new features and security patches
- Update themes/plugins if compatible versions are released
- Renew domain name and hosting at least 1-2 weeks before expiration
- Back up files/database in case restore is needed
- Monitor site speed/traffic to catch problems
- Test functionality across devices/browsers

Plan dates every 1 to 3 months to perform an overall health check, apply any updates, create backups and scan for broken links or issues. This website maintenance keeps everything running smoothly.

Understanding HTML and CSS Basics

While a CMS handles much of the heavy lifting, knowing some basic HTML and CSS skills allows deeper customization in the code behind your site.

HTML Building Blocks

HTML provides the overall structure and semantics through tags like:

- <h1> to <h6> - Heading levels
- <p> - Paragraph text
- <img> - Images
- <nav> - Navigation links
- <article> - Blog post/article content
- <form> - Forms

HTML is the skeleton everything else gets built upon. This is just a simple example of how to put together an HTML page. The first screenshot is the code that's used:

```
1   <!DOCTYPE html>
2   <html>
3   <head>
4   <title>Page Title</title>
5   </head>
6   <body>
7
8   <h1>This is a Heading. It's an "h1"</h1>
9   <p>This is a paragraph. These tags provide a way to display text in a way that looks
    like it is natural.</p>
10  <br>
11  <h2>This is a Heading. It's an "h2"</h2>
12  <br>
13  <h3>This is a Heading. It's an "h3"</h3>
14  <br>
15  <h4>This is a Heading. It's an "h4"</h4>
16  <br>
17  <h5>This is a Heading. It's an "h5"</h5>
18  <br>
19  <h6>This is a Heading. It's an "h6"</h6>
20  <br>
21  <h7>This is a Heading. It's an "h7"</h7>
22  <p>As you can see the "h7" is not really a heading.  The h7 is a phony tag and doesn't
    exist. You can try it, but to no avail. ;~) </p>
23  <br>
24  </body>
25  </html>
```

This is the page as it appears in the browser:

This is a Heading. It's an "h1"

This is a paragraph. These tags provide a way to display text in a way that looks like it is natural.

This is a Heading. It's an "h2"

This is a Heading. It's an "h3"

This is a Heading. It's an "h4"

This is a Heading. It's an "h5"

This is a Heading. It's an "h6"

This is a Heading. It's an "h7"

As you can see the "h7" is not really a heading. The h7 is a phony tag and doesn't exist. You can try it, but to no avail. ;~)

Styling Sites with Cascading Style Sheets (CSS)

CSS gives a webpage a visual design like:

- Color - Fonts, backgrounds, links
- Text - Styles, sizes, alignment
- Layout - Padding, margins, float (switching between desktop and mobile), grid
- Responsiveness - Media queries
- Effects - Shadows, animations

While I was going to give you an example of the above page with CSS added, I'm not going to do that. This is being done for two reasons:
- I suck at CSS, well let me rephrase that, every time I try to do something with CSS I have to look up every step.
- CSS is easy to learn if you want to do so. W3School has a great course on it. You would be much better served to follow this link (https://www.w3schools.com/w3css/defaulT.asp) and look at some examples.

Without CSS, HTML would be more like plain unformatted text. It is a best practice to separate the design elements from the content elements as much as possible. By putting the design into CSS stylesheets, there is flexibility in the design that can allow for changes as the site is built.

Learning HTML and CSS empowers deeper customization. Even rudimentary knowledge unlocks more possibilities to:

- Tweak templates
- Create custom landing pages
- Craft complex grid layouts
- Dial in responsive breakpoints
- Craft smart interactive animations

Beautiful websites can be built without the need to learn CSS. Learning CSS, however, will help you refine things so that the customizations will be yours, and add your signature to the site.

As a final note, do as I say, don't do as I do. I would feel better about myself if I were to learn CSS, the problem is that quite honestly my family doesn't need me to feel better about myself.

Difference Between WordPress.org and WordPress.com

WordPress is a popular content management system (CMS) that powers millions of websites worldwide. It comes in two primary flavors: WordPress.org and WordPress.com. Understanding the differences between these two can help users choose the platform that best fits their needs.

WordPress.org

WordPress.org is often referred to as the "self-hosted WordPress." It is a free, open-source software that you can download and install on your own web server.

This seems a bit misleading. WordPress.org is where you get the software that will make up your WordPress website. This will also be one place to get amazing community help and answers to questions that you may have at times. You may never go to WordPress.org, but I would recommend creating a free login account. This will allow you to have access to all of the free benefits of membership.

Here are the key features and considerations:

- **Flexibility and Control:** With WordPress.org, you have full control over your website. You can customize it extensively, add any theme or plugin you want, and modify the code to your heart's content.
- **Cost:** While the WordPress software itself is free, you need to pay for hosting and domain registration. Costs can vary based on the hosting provider and your website's requirements.
- **Maintenance:** You are responsible for maintaining your website. This includes

backups, security updates, and installing updates for WordPress, themes, and plugins.
- **Monetization:** You have the freedom to monetize your website in any way you choose, including ads, affiliate marketing, and selling products or services.

WordPress.com

WordPress.com is a hosted platform that runs on WordPress software. It's a more hands-off approach to website building and hosting, managed by Automattic. Here's what sets WordPress.com apart:

- **Ease of Use:** WordPress.com takes care of hosting, security, backups, and updates. This makes it easier for beginners or those who prefer not to deal with the technical aspects of running a website.
- **Pricing:** It offers a basic free plan with WordPress.com branding. Paid plans are available, which provide more features, the ability to use a custom domain, and removal of WordPress.com ads.
- **Limitations:** The free and lower-tier plans have limitations on customization. You cannot upload custom themes or plugins unless you are on a Business plan or higher. This can limit your website's functionality and appearance.
- **Monetization:** Restrictions also apply to monetization options. On the free and lower-tier plans, you cannot run your own ads. With higher-tiered plans, you gain more flexibility,

but WordPress.com still has more restrictions compared to a self-hosted WordPress.org site.

Conclusion

The choice between WordPress.org and WordPress.com depends on your needs, skills, and the level of control you want over your website. If you're looking for complete freedom to customize your site, don't mind handling the technical aspects, and are willing to invest in hosting, WordPress.org is the better choice.

On the other hand, if you prefer a more straightforward, less technical approach, with hosting and maintenance taken care of for you, WordPress.com offers a convenient solution, especially for beginners.

Chapter 6: Going Live and Beyond

Congratulations - at this point your domain is registered, web hosting is set up, and website content is ready to be created or already created. Now it's time for the exciting part - officially launching your site live on the internet!

This chapter covers crucial steps like publishing your site publicly, vital post-launch tasks like submissions to search engines, and long-term website maintenance best practices. We'll also discuss common issues that crop up with new sites and how to address them.

By the end of this chapter, you'll know how to put your website live, have a process for monitoring and optimizing site performance, and be prepared to scale up your infrastructure as site traffic inevitably grows. Launching is just the first step - maintaining momentum requires vigilance.

Let's get your site off the ground successfully!

Publishing Your Website

When your website development is complete, publishing it makes the site live and visible to the whole world:

Choose a Launch Date

Give yourself a concrete deadline to work towards. Building anticipation also helps drive initial traffic. It's also a good idea to allow a 1-2 week buffer for any final tweaks.

Test Everything First

Thoroughly test all pages and functionality on both desktop and mobile. Friends/family can provide feedback and help identify any issues before your public launch date.

If pieces like Contact Forms were disabled earlier, make sure to fully enable them prior to launch.
A plethora of form plugins in WordPress serve as mechanisms allowing clients to reach out to you, regarding your website or the commodities and amenities you provide. However, it's worth noting that the only foolproof way to avoid spamming through the form is to eliminate the form completely.

Certain groups perceive it their duty to inundate your website with numerous harmful and perilous links. Remember, disabling the commenting feature on blog posts and articles is an efficient method to halt the propagation of these hazardous phishing/spam/miscellaneous links.

Picture a scenario where individuals equipped with such proficiency and flair in programming and automation utilized their expertise to combat global issues like hunger, warfare, disease, and poverty. Imagine the swift resolution of these world problems. Then time travel to a place in your imagination where such a world is confined to a lightless room, the key misplaced, and never revisited. This will bring you back to reality. Turning a blind eye towards those lacking ethics won't make them disappear, however, knowing that they exist and taking precautions will help us all sleep better.

Check out appendix A for some great information about understanding phishing and scams. Be prepared.

Promoting Your Website Launch

Get Ready, Get Set...Promote! Why marketing should begin at launch…

You invest significant time and resources getting a website designed, built, tested and hosted. But without promotion driving visitors to see your shiny new creation, it risks whirling in obscurity rather than realizing its purpose.

While I am probably one of the worst marketing gurus to listen to, this is at least exploring some other options that are out there. It is definitely beyond the scope of this book, but marketing your site might at least get some pats on the back, and some of your family may get a kick out of it.

Effective launch marketing generates that initial momentum that can propel a site from unknown to respected authority and community anchor. First impressions set the foundation and expectations that are harder to reset later.

With the web overflowing with competing content, building even basic awareness as a newcomer is supremely challenging though. Cutting through the clutter requires deploying a promotional mix of both mass reach and precision targeting.

This section outlines impactful strategies for gaining visibility leveraging social media, email, PR, advertising, partnerships and more. Deploying a multi-channel promotional blitz maximizes discovery while identifying what resonates most with your audience.

Let's explore methods for alerting the world to your freshly launched online presence! Without promotion, no visitors will come, so we'll address how to spread the word far and wide.

Driving visitors to a fledgling site takes creativity and persistence. Combining multiple promotions is key for launch success.

1. **Social Media Campaigns:** Utilize social media platforms to tease the launch with sneak peeks, countdowns, and launch day announcements. Consider paid promotions to target your ideal audience effectively.

2. **Email Marketing:** Send out an email blast to your existing subscribers announcing the launch date, and follow up with a launch day email. Highlight key features or content that will interest your audience.

3. **Press Release:** Craft a compelling press release about your website's launch and distribute it to relevant media outlets. This can increase your reach and add an aura of professionalism to your launch.

4. **Collaborations and Influencer Partnerships:** Partner with influencers or brands in your niche to promote your website. Their endorsement can lend credibility and attract their followers to your site.

5. **Launch Event:** Host a virtual launch event or webinar to showcase your new website. Offer a tour of the site, highlight its features, and answer live questions from the audience.

6. **Content Marketing:** Create valuable content that draws people to your new website. Blog posts, videos, infographics, and guides related to your niche can attract organic traffic.

7. **Search Engine Optimization (SEO):** Optimize your website's content with relevant keywords to ensure it ranks well on search engine results pages (SERPs), making it easier for your target audience to find you.

8. **Special Promotions:** Offer launch-specific promotions, such as discounts, free trials, or exclusive content, to encourage people to visit and explore your new website.

By strategically promoting your website's launch, you can maximize its initial impact, attract a substantial audience, and set the stage for sustained growth.

Remember, the goal is not just to launch with a bang but to maintain momentum and continue engaging your audience long after the initial excitement fades.

Following this publishing process, you can confidently open your polished website up to the world knowing everything works as intended for visitors discovery!

Sustaining awareness after launch is challenging but deploying a diverse combination of owned, earned and paid marketing provides the exposure that can turn visitors into loyal community members.

Which promotional strategies resonate most depends on your specific brand and audience. Testing into what works allows doubling down on the highest traction channels.

Reaching The Finish Line

And with that, you now have all the building blocks needed to get a professional website successfully online - domain, hosting, site construction, launch, and growth.

This guide walked you step-by-step through the core foundations like:

- Understanding domain name registration
- Configuring DNS settings
- Comparing web hosting providers
- Building sites on CMS platforms
- Customizing templates and themes
- Publishing live with testing and promotion
- Expanding reach through organic and paid channels

While the little details and decisions along the way may shift, the roadmap for creating an effective online presence remains largely constant.

The internet opens unlimited possibilities to share your passions, build communities, help others, spread ideas, and grow businesses. So let your website be the jumping off point to start realizing dreams and leaving your positive mark on the world.

Appendix A: Understanding Phishing and Scams

This appendix is written by Brandon Wright (of Arshem.com, a design agency that offers web hosting, development and design services to a select group of clients.) Brandon been in hosting and development for more than a decade and has run the gamut of issues with protecting the sites and information of his customers. He has graciously writen this special section to help people make the best of their sites.

Understanding Phishing and Scams

Phishing and scams are prevalent cyber threats that aim to deceive individuals and organizations to steal sensitive information or money. By understanding their definitions, key characteristics, and types, we can better protect ourselves against these malicious activities.

Definition and Key Characteristics of Phishing and Scams

Phishing is a type of cyberattack where attackers impersonate legitimate entities to trick individuals into revealing personal information such as usernames, passwords, and credit card numbers. These attacks often occur through emails, websites, or text messages that appear to be from trusted sources.

Scams, more broadly, refer to deceptive schemes or tricks used to defraud people. While phishing is a specific type of scam that uses digital means to deceive, scams can take various forms, including phone calls, fake advertisements, and fraudulent websites.

Key characteristics of phishing and scams include:

- **Deception**: Both rely on convincing the target that the interaction is legitimate.
- **Urgency**: Messages often create a sense of urgency, such as threats of account closure or missed opportunities, to prompt immediate action.
- **Social Engineering**: Attackers exploit human psychology to manipulate victims into providing sensitive information or taking harmful actions.
- **Impersonation:** Phishers and scammers impersonate trusted entities, such as banks, government agencies, or well-known companies, to gain trust.
- **Common Types of Phishing and Scams**
- **Email Phishing:** Attackers send emails that appear to be from legitimate sources, such as banks or online services, asking recipients to click on a link or download an attachment. The link usually leads to a fake website that

captures login credentials, or the attachment contains malware.
- **Deceptive Pop-ups:** These pop-ups appear while browsing the web and claim to be from legitimate software companies. They often warn of a virus infection and prompt the user to download a fake antivirus program, which is actually malware.
- **Spear Phishing:** A more targeted form of phishing, spear phishing involves personalized emails sent to specific individuals or organizations. The messages often contain information that makes them seem credible, such as the recipient's name, job title, or recent activities.
- **Whaling:** A type of spear phishing that targets high-profile individuals within an organization, such as executives or other decision-makers. The aim is to steal sensitive data or initiate unauthorized financial transactions.
- **Lottery Scams:** Victims receive notifications that they have won a lottery or sweepstakes they never entered. To claim the prize, they are asked to provide personal information or pay a fee upfront.
- **Tech Support Scams:** Scammers pose as tech support agents from reputable companies and convince victims that their computer is infected with malware. They then offer to fix the

non-existent issue for a fee or gain remote access to steal information.
- **Vishing (Voice Phishing):** Attackers use phone calls to impersonate legitimate entities, such as banks or government agencies, to extract personal information or financial details.

The Impact of Phishing and Scams on Users and Businesses

The consequences of phishing and scams can be severe for both individuals and organizations:

- **Financial Loss:** Victims may lose money directly through fraudulent transactions or indirectly by having their financial information stolen and misused.
- **Identity Theft:** Personal information obtained through phishing can be used to commit identity theft, leading to long-term financial and legal problems for the victim.
- **Data Breaches:** Businesses targeted by phishing attacks may suffer data breaches, exposing sensitive customer information and damaging their reputation.
- **Operational Disruption:** Scams and phishing attacks can disrupt business operations, especially if they involve ransomware or other forms of malware.
- **Legal Consequences:** Organizations that fail to protect their data can face legal action and

regulatory fines, particularly if they violate data protection laws.
- **Emotional Distress:** Victims of scams and phishing may experience stress, anxiety, and a loss of trust in digital communications.

Best Practices for Website Safety

Ensuring the safety and security of a website is crucial to protect both the site's data and its users from cyber threats. Implementing robust security measures can significantly reduce the risk of attacks such as phishing, malware infections, and unauthorized access. Here are some best practices for maintaining website safety:

- Implementing Secure Protocols such as HTTPS and SSL/TLS Certificates
- **HTTPS (Hypertext Transfer Protocol Secure)** is an extension of HTTP that provides secure communication over a computer network. When a website uses HTTPS, the data transmitted between the user's browser and the web server is encrypted, ensuring confidentiality and integrity.
- **SSL/TLS Certificates:** Secure Sockets Layer (SSL) and its successor, Transport Layer Security (TLS), are cryptographic protocols that secure data transmitted over the internet.

Obtaining and installing an SSL/TLS certificate for your website enables HTTPS, which helps protect sensitive information, such as login credentials and payment details, from being intercepted by attackers.

Best Practices:
- Always use HTTPS for all pages on your website, not just those that handle sensitive information.
- Obtain an SSL/TLS certificate from a trusted certificate authority (CA).
- Regularly check the validity of your SSL/TLS certificates and renew them before they expire.
- Use strong encryption standards (e.g., TLS 1.2 or higher).
- **Regularly Updating and Patching Website Software, Plugins, and Themes**
- Keeping all website components up to date is vital to prevent security vulnerabilities.

Best Practices:
- Regularly update your content management system (CMS), such as WordPress, Joomla, or Drupal.
- Update all plugins, themes, and third-party software used on your website.
- Subscribe to security alerts for your CMS and plugins to stay informed about new vulnerabilities and updates.

- Apply security patches promptly to fix known vulnerabilities.
- Utilizing Strong, Unique Passwords and Implementing Two-Factor Authentication (2FA)
- Passwords are a primary defense mechanism for securing user accounts and administrative access.

Best Practices:

<u>Use strong passwords that are at least 12 characters long, including a mix of letters, numbers, and special characters.</u>
Avoid using easily guessable information such as common words, phrases, or personal details.

- Implement two-factor authentication (2FA) to add an extra layer of security. This requires users to provide a second form of verification (e.g., a code sent to their mobile device) in addition to their password.
- Encourage users to use password managers to generate and store unique passwords securely.
- Configuring Proper Website Backups and Disaster Recovery Plans
- Backups are essential for recovering from data loss incidents caused by cyberattacks, hardware failures, or human errors.
- Best Practices:
- Regularly back up your website, including databases, files, and configurations.

- Store backups in multiple locations, such as on-site, off-site, and in the cloud.
- Test backups periodically to ensure they can be successfully restored.
- Develop a disaster recovery plan that outlines the steps to take in case of a website compromise or data loss event.
- Educating Users on Website Safety, Phishing, and Scams
- Educating users about potential threats and safe practices can significantly enhance overall website security.

Best Practices:
- Provide resources and training materials on recognizing and avoiding phishing attacks and scams.
- Regularly update users on new security threats and best practices for staying safe online.
- Implement security awareness programs that include phishing simulations to help users identify and respond to suspicious activities.
- Encourage users to report any suspicious emails, messages, or activities related to the website.
- By adopting these best practices for website safety, you can create a secure online environment that protects both your website and its users from a variety of cyber threats. Implementing secure protocols, keeping

software updated, using strong authentication methods, ensuring regular backups, and educating users are all essential steps in maintaining robust website security.

Protecting Your Website from Phishing Attacks

- Phishing attacks can be highly detrimental, both to your website and its users. By implementing proactive security measures, you can significantly reduce the risk of such attacks. Here are some strategies to protect your website from phishing:
- Identifying and Removing Potential Phishing Vectors on Your Website
- Phishing vectors are points of entry or features that attackers can exploit to execute phishing attacks.
- Best Practices:
- Suspicious Forms: Regularly audit forms on your website to ensure they are necessary, secure, and do not request sensitive information unless absolutely needed. Use CAPTCHA to prevent automated submissions and validate form inputs to avoid code injection attacks.

- Unverified Third-Party Integrations: Review all third-party integrations and plugins to ensure they come from reputable sources. Remove any that are no longer in use or have been identified as potential security risks. Always keep them updated to the latest versions.
- Cross-Site Scripting (XSS): Implement Content Security Policy (CSP) headers to prevent XSS attacks. Ensure input fields are properly sanitized and encoded to prevent malicious scripts from being executed on your site.
- Employing Email Verification and Spam Filtering Solutions
- Phishing often begins with deceptive emails that lure users to malicious websites or convince them to disclose sensitive information.

Best Practices:

Email Verification: Use email verification tools to check the legitimacy of email addresses registering on your site. These tools can help reduce spam and prevent phishing emails from being sent using fake or invalid addresses.

- Spam Filtering: Implement robust spam filtering solutions to identify and block phishing emails before they reach users. Utilize spam filters provided by email service providers, and consider additional third-party spam filtering services.

- Educate Users: Train users to recognize suspicious emails and avoid clicking on links or downloading attachments from unknown sources.
- Utilizing Domain-based Message Authentication, Reporting, and Conformance (DMARC) to Prevent Email Spoofing
- DMARC is an email authentication protocol that helps prevent attackers from spoofing your domain.
- Best Practices:
- SPF (Sender Policy Framework): Publish an SPF record that specifies which mail servers are authorized to send emails on behalf of your domain. This helps email recipients verify that incoming messages are from your legitimate servers.
- DKIM (DomainKeys Identified Mail): Use DKIM to add a digital signature to your emails, verifying that the message content has not been altered in transit and confirming the sender's identity.
- DMARC Policy: Implement a DMARC policy that specifies how email receivers should handle unauthenticated emails. Start with a "none" policy to monitor email traffic and then gradually move to "quarantine" or "reject" policies as you gain confidence in your setup.

Regularly review DMARC reports to identify and mitigate any spoofing attempts.
- Monitoring and Analyzing Website Traffic to Detect Anomalies and Potential Phishing Attacks
- Continuous monitoring of website traffic can help detect unusual activities that may indicate phishing attempts.

Best Practices:
- Web Application Firewall (WAF): Deploy a WAF to filter and monitor HTTP traffic between your website and the internet. A WAF can block malicious traffic, including automated bots and known attack patterns.
- Intrusion Detection Systems (IDS): Use IDS to detect and respond to potential security breaches. IDS tools can analyze traffic patterns and alert you to anomalies that may indicate phishing or other attacks.
- Traffic Analysis: Regularly analyze website traffic logs for unusual patterns, such as spikes in traffic from specific IP addresses, unusual login attempts, or sudden changes in user behavior. Tools like Google Analytics and specialized security analytics platforms can help you track and analyze traffic.
- User Behavior Analytics (UBA): Implement UBA to monitor and analyze user activities on your website. UBA can identify deviations from

normal behavior that may indicate a compromised account or phishing attack.
-
- Protecting your website from phishing attacks requires a multifaceted approach that involves securing potential entry points, verifying and filtering emails, implementing authentication protocols, and continuously monitoring website traffic. By adopting these strategies, you can create a robust defense against phishing and ensure the safety and integrity of your website and its users.

Safeguarding Users Against Scams

Ensuring user safety on your website is crucial to maintain trust and integrity. By proactively verifying and monitoring user-generated content, establishing clear policies, and providing tools and resources, you can protect users from scams and fraudulent activities.

- Verifying and Monitoring User-Generated Content
- User-generated content, such as reviews, comments, and forum posts, can be a common target for scammers looking to exploit unsuspecting users.

Best Practices:

Automated Filters: Implement automated filters to detect and block potentially harmful content. Use machine learning algorithms to identify patterns associated with scams, such as suspicious links, repetitive posting, and specific keywords.

- Manual Moderation: Complement automated systems with manual moderation to review flagged content. Employ a team of moderators to check for false positives and ensure nuanced, context-sensitive evaluation of content.
- User Verification: Require users to verify their identities before they can post content. Verification can include email confirmation, phone number validation, or linking to social media profiles.
- Regular Audits: Perform regular audits of user-generated content to identify and remove any content that violates your guidelines or poses a risk to users.
- Establishing Clear Guidelines and Policies
- Having clear and enforceable guidelines helps prevent scams and provides a framework for taking action against malicious activities.

Best Practices:

- User Guidelines: Create comprehensive user guidelines that outline acceptable behavior and the types of content that are prohibited. Make these guidelines easily accessible on your website.

- Vendor and Advertiser Policies: Establish strict policies for vendors and advertisers to ensure they operate transparently and ethically. Require vendors to provide accurate product descriptions and to honor their return and refund policies.
- Enforcement Mechanisms: Develop mechanisms to enforce your policies, such as account suspension or termination for users, vendors, or advertisers who violate your guidelines. Ensure that enforcement actions are consistent and well-documented.
- Transparency: Be transparent about your policies and enforcement actions. Provide a clear process for users to appeal decisions or report policy violations.
- Implementing Trust Indicators
- Trust indicators help users identify legitimate and trustworthy content, products, and services on your website.

Best Practices:
- Verified Badges: Use verified badges to highlight accounts that have been authenticated. For example, assign badges to verified vendors, advertisers, and users who have completed identity verification processes.
- Customer Reviews: Display customer reviews and ratings prominently on product pages. Ensure that reviews are genuine by verifying

the identities of reviewers and using algorithms to detect fake reviews.
- Transparent Business Information: Provide clear and detailed information about your business, including contact details, physical address, and company background. Display trust seals or certifications from reputable third parties to reinforce your credibility.
- Secure Payment Methods: Offer secure payment methods and provide guarantees for transactions. Highlight secure payment options and outline refund and dispute resolution processes.
- Providing Users with Resources and Tools
- Empowering users with the knowledge and tools to recognize and report scams is vital for maintaining a safe online environment.

Best Practices:
- Educational Resources: Create and disseminate educational materials that teach users how to identify and avoid scams. Include information on common scam tactics and provide examples of fraudulent messages or advertisements.
- Reporting Tools: Implement easy-to-use tools that allow users to report suspicious activity, content, or transactions. Ensure that reports are reviewed promptly and take appropriate action to address the issues.

- Help and Support: Offer dedicated customer support channels for users to seek help if they encounter scams. Provide timely assistance and guidance on how to handle potential scams or fraudulent activities.
- Regular Updates: Keep users informed about new scams and threats. Regularly update your educational resources and communicate any changes to your policies or reporting mechanisms.

Safeguarding users against scams requires a combination of proactive content verification, clear policies, trust indicators, and user education. By implementing these best practices, you can create a secure online environment that fosters trust and protects users from fraudulent activities. This approach not only enhances user safety but also strengthens the reputation and integrity of your website.

The Future of Website Safety

As cyber threats continue to evolve, the future of website safety hinges on the adoption of advanced technologies, adherence to industry standards, and the cultivation of a proactive security culture. Here's a look at the emerging trends and strategies that will shape the future of website safety.

Emerging Trends and Technologies in Website Safety

AI-Powered Security Solutions:

Machine Learning Algorithms: AI and machine learning can analyze vast amounts of data to detect patterns and anomalies indicative of cyber threats. These technologies can help identify new types of attacks and respond in real-time.

Behavioral Analysis: AI can monitor user behavior to detect unusual activities that may signal an attack. For example, sudden changes in login patterns or transaction behaviors can trigger alerts for further investigation.

Automated Threat Response: AI can automate responses to detected threats, such as isolating compromised systems, blocking malicious traffic, and applying patches or updates.

Biometric Authentication:

Enhanced Security: Biometric authentication, such as fingerprint scanning, facial recognition, and voice recognition, provides a higher level of security compared to traditional passwords. It is harder for attackers to replicate biometric data.

User Convenience: Biometrics offer a more seamless and user-friendly authentication experience, reducing reliance on complex passwords and improving user adoption of security measures.

Blockchain Technology:

Decentralized Security: Blockchain technology can provide a decentralized approach to securing data, making it more difficult for attackers to alter records without detection.

Smart Contracts: Smart contracts can automate and secure transactions by executing predefined conditions, reducing the risk of fraud and ensuring data integrity.

Zero Trust Architecture:

Continuous Verification: Zero Trust principles require continuous verification of users and devices, regardless of their location within or outside the network. This minimizes the risk of insider threats and unauthorized access.

Least Privilege Access: Implementing least privilege access ensures that users and applications have only the minimum level of access necessary to perform their functions, reducing the attack surface.

The Role of Industry Standards, Regulations, and Collaborative Efforts

Industry Standards:

Adopting Best Practices: Adherence to industry standards, such as the ISO/IEC 27001 for information security management and the NIST Cybersecurity Framework, helps organizations implement robust security measures.

Compliance: Compliance with standards ensures that organizations follow established guidelines for securing data and systems, which can reduce vulnerabilities and enhance trust among users.

Regulations:

Data Protection Laws: Regulations such as the General Data Protection Regulation (GDPR) and the California Consumer Privacy Act (CCPA) impose strict requirements on how organizations handle personal data, driving improvements in data security practices.

Cybersecurity Legislation: Emerging cybersecurity legislation mandates proactive measures to protect critical infrastructure and sensitive information, ensuring that organizations prioritize security in their operations.

Collaborative Efforts:

Information Sharing: Collaboration between organizations, industry groups, and government agencies is essential for sharing threat intelligence and best practices. Platforms like Information Sharing and Analysis Centers (ISACs) facilitate this exchange.

Joint Initiatives: Collaborative initiatives, such as public-private partnerships and industry consortia, can drive the development of innovative security solutions and promote a unified approach to combating cyber threats.

Preparing for an Evolving Threat Landscape and Fostering a Security-First Culture

Continuous Monitoring and Adaptation:

Threat Intelligence: Stay informed about the latest cyber threats and vulnerabilities through threat intelligence services and regular security assessments.

Adaptive Security: Implement adaptive security measures that can evolve in response to emerging threats. This includes regular updates to security protocols, software, and hardware.

Security Awareness and Training:

Employee Training: Regularly train employees on cybersecurity best practices, recognizing phishing attempts, and responding to security incidents.

User Education: Educate users about safe online behaviors and the importance of security measures, such as strong passwords and two-factor authentication.

Security-First Culture:

Leadership Commitment: Ensure that organizational leadership prioritizes cybersecurity and allocates resources to implement effective security measures.

Integrated Security: Integrate security into all aspects of the organization's operations, from development and IT to marketing and customer support.

Proactive Approach: Foster a proactive approach to security by encouraging continuous improvement, regular audits, and a commitment to staying ahead of potential threats.

The future of website safety will be shaped by the integration of advanced technologies, adherence to industry standards, and a collaborative, proactive approach to cybersecurity. By embracing AI-powered solutions, biometric authentication, and zero trust principles, organizations can enhance their defenses against evolving threats. Additionally, fostering a security-first culture and engaging in collaborative efforts will ensure that organizations are well-prepared to protect their websites and users from emerging cyber threats.

Talking a bit about the passwords:

https://www.security.org/how-secure-is-my-password/

This website is a site that will take your input and evaluate how long it would take to break the password using a computer program.

Here is what I have found:

notiwhatyour -12 lower case letters - 3 weeks to break

notIwhatYour - upper and lower case letters - 300 years to break

notiwhatyourout - 15 lower case - 1000 years

notiwhatyouroUT - 15 letters 2 upper - 43 million years to break

n0t1whatyouroUT - 15 letters caps and lower w/ 2 numbers - 2 trillion years to break n0t1whatyouroUT% - 16 characters one special character - 1 trillion years to break

With WordPress you can use spaces in your password, it is considered a special character. Here is what I am going to check:

CleverLittleTerror - 6 trillion years (6 followed by 9 - zeroes)

Clever Little Terror - 8 quintillion years (8 followed by 18 zeroes)

Clever Little Terror 9 - 7 hundred sextillion years (700 followed by 21 years)

Need I say more about making passwords that are tough to break? That site above it rather fun to play with. Check out how simple it is to create passwords that very difficult to guess or even hammer into submission.

Glossary

Bandwidth - The volume of data transfer capacity available for a website and hosting account to handle traffic, measured in gigabytes (GB).

Cache/Caching - Temporarily storing website files, assets and data in memory to accelerate speed accessing and loading that content again. Helps improve site performance.

CDN - Content Delivery Network - A distributed global network with edge locations for caching content closer to users. This speeds the delivery of assets and media. Popular CDNs include CloudFlare, Akamai and Amazon CloudFront.

CMS - Content Management System - Software for building, organizing and managing website content and structure through administration interfaces. Popular platforms are WordPress, Joomla and Drupal.

cPanel - A common web hosting control panel interface for managing servers, including domains, files, databases, email configurations and settings.

CSS - Cascading Style Sheets - A stylesheet coding language controlling presentation and visual styling of elements on web pages that are written in HTML.

Dashboard - The administrative backend interface of hosting, domain and CMS platforms where all site management, tools and settings are handled. Provides oversight and controls.

Dedicated Hosting - A physical server allocated solely for use by one website or company. Resources are not shared, providing higher performance, control and security. More expensive than shared hosting.

DNS - Domain Name System - The backbone "phonebook directory" of the internet that resolves human-readable domain names into computer-usable IP addresses, enabling routing to sites and services.

DNS resolver - A type of DNS server that receives domain name requests from web browsers and other internet-connected clients, asks other DNS servers to find the IP address associated with that domain name through recursive lookups if required, caches the results, and returns the IP address answer to the clients to enable routing connections.

Domain - The unique human-readable name that identifies and represents a specific website or web address online, like company.com. Registered through a domain registrar.

Domain Privacy - An option when registering domains that masks the registrant's personal information from public view in WHOIS records which are replaced with proxy contact details instead for anonymity.

Domain Registrar - Company authorized and accredited to officially register domain names to customers and sells annual domain registrations to end users through reseller channels. Popular options include GoDaddy, Namecheap and Bluehost.

FTP - File Transfer Protocol - Technical standard protocol defining how files are exchanged over network connections. Used commonly for uploading website files from a computer to web servers.

HTML - Hypertext Markup Language - Standard coding language creating the base structure and content of web pages through tags and elements made visible on browsers. Required building block for all websites.

HTTP - Hypertext Transfer Protocol - Foundation protocol of the world wide web that defines communication standards between web browsers and servers, allowing accessing inter-linked resources across the internet. Based on request/response messaging.

HTTPS - Hypertext Transfer Protocol Secure - The protocol for secure communication over a network, that encrypts and protects internet traffic and connections through SSL/TLS certificates. Enables secure transfers and transactions, URL padlocks, identity assurance. The S at the end signifies enhanced security compared to standard unencrypted HTTP.

IaaS - Infrastructure-as-a-Service - Provisioning scalable, flexible technology infrastructure like storage capacity, virtual machines/servers and networking components using cloud computing on an as-needed basis avoiding capital expenditures. Enables dynamically meeting needs.

IP Address - An assigned numerical string that identifies and allows locating a specific device or server connected to any network using the internet protocol for communications between machines.

MX records - A type of DNS record that routes and delivers email to mail servers using routing preferences by pointing domain names to mail transport server IP addresses. One of the core DNS record types.

PaaS - Platform-as-a-Service - A category of cloud computing services providing a full managed platform application stack and software building tools hosted in the cloud, avoiding need to install or invest in underlying infrastructure and resources locally. Focus is solely on the application and data requirements.

SaaS - Software-as-a-Service - A cloud computing model offering access to ready-made software and hosted applications over the internet through subscription plans removing need for upfront licensing, data center requirements or manual installations onto each user device. All maintenance and updates also handled by the SaaS vendor.

Shared Hosting - Most common and cost-effective standard web hosting option in which many accounts reside together on the same server collectively sharing bandwidth, disk space, data transfer allowances, and other computing resources efficiently due to low utilization per site.

SSL Certificate - Encryption certificates helping secure website data transmission through HTTPS protocol by facilitating encrypted links and enabling browser address bar padlocks and other trust signals. SSL certs encrypt communication between browsers and servers protecting privacy.

Web Host - Company providing web servers, storage, network capacity, dedicated resources and associated technologies required for live websites and applications connected to and accessible through the internet. Offer hosting across varying plans from shared reseller to dedicated servers.

WHOIS - Public record database listing contact details and registration information of domain holders and assignees including registrant names, addresses and phone numbers. Allows identifying owners of internet properties through these lookup records.
There are 12 root servers that control, and direct traffic to domain names all over the world.

The root servers are operated by 12 different organizations:

      A VeriSign Global Registry Services
      B University of Southern California, Information Sciences Institute
      C Cogent Communications
      D University of Maryland

E NASA Ames Research Center
F Internet Systems Consortium, Inc.
G US DoD Network Information Center
H US Army Research Lab
I Netnod
J VeriSign Global Registry Services
K RIPE NCC
L ICANN
M WIDE Project

www.ingramcontent.com/pod-product-compliance
Lightning Source LLC
Chambersburg PA
CBHW072050230526
45479CB00010B/644